Britain in the Past
The
Bronze Age

Moira Butterfield

W

Franklin Watts
Published in 2017 by the Watts Publishing Group

Editor: Sarah Ridley
Editor in chief: John C. Miles
Series designer: Jane Hawkins
Art director: Peter Scoulding
Picture research: Diana Morris

Picture credits:
Bally Stock/Robert Harding PL: 27t. Alena Brozova/Dreamstime: 10b. cornfield/Shutterstock: 12b.
© DNPA: 20c, 21t, 21b. Annie Eagle/Alamy: 22b. Diane Earl: 24b. Mark Eaton/Dreamstime: 1, 4tl,
6tl, 8tl, 10tl, 11, 12tl, 14tl, 16tl, 18tl, 20tl, 22tl, 24tl, 26tl, 28tl. Nick Edwards: 16b. © Found by
Andy Elliott of SWMAG/www.swmag.org : 17t. Gallo Images/Getty Images: 8b. Chris Howes Wild
Places/Alamy: 9. Last Refuge/Robert Harding PL: front cover, 28b. J Miles: 6c. National Museums
Scotland: 13. National Museum Wales: 26c, 27b. Dmitry Naumov/Dreamstime: 7c. Andreas Praefcke/
CC Wikimedia Commons: 15b. Skyscan photolibrary/Alamy: 14c. Stocker1970/Dreamstime: 7t. Derek
Stone/ Alamy: 18b. Trindhøj National Museum of Denmark: 23. Wessex Archaeology: 4b, 5t, 5b.
Den Whitton/CC wikipedia: 25. Adam Woolfit/Robert Harding PL/Superstock: 19t. C M Dixon/AAA
Collection/Alamy: 29.

*Every attempt has been made to clear copyright. Should there be any inadvertent
omission please apply to the publisher for rectification.*

Dewey number: 941

ISBN: 978 1 4451 4059 9

Printed in China

Franklin Watts
An imprint of
Hachette Children's Group
Part of The Watts Publishing Group
Carmelite House
50 Victoria Embankment
London EC4Y 0DZ

An Hachette UK Company
www.hachette.co.uk

www.franklinwatts.co.uk

FSC
www.fsc.org

MIX
Paper from
responsible sources
FSC® C104740

Contents

Bringer of gold

Occasionally an invention comes along that completely changes the way that people live. Around 4,300 years ago people in Britain learned how to make and work with metal. We call this the beginning of the Bronze Age.

Metal man

Up until around 2300 BCE people lived in what we call the Stone Age. They used stone tools made from pieces of flint and didn't know how to create metal. Then new arrivals brought the skill from mainland Europe. The grave of one of these new metal maestros has been found at Amesbury in Wiltshire. We call him the Amesbury Archer because he was buried with lots of arrowheads for hunting, as well as metal objects.

◀ The Amesbury Archer in position in his grave, surrounded by objects.

Rolled gold

The Amesbury Archer was buried with clothes, hunting equipment, pots and tools. Perhaps his friends thought he might need them in an afterlife. One of his tools was a cushion stone, a flat stone used like a tiny workbench for working on metal shapes. There were also small rolled pieces of gold, the first ever gold found in Britain. It's thought the archer might have worn these in his hair.

A rolled gold shape, perhaps worn over a lock of hair. ▼

Alpine arrival

Scientists can analyse teeth to discover where someone grew up. We know from this work that the archer came from the Alps, near modern-day Switzerland. When he arrived in Britain locals must have found his metalworking skills amazing and marvelled at the gold he wore.

5

See some mysteries

The Amesbury Archer lived in the era we call the early Bronze Age. There are lots of mysterious big monuments dating from this time, but we can only guess how they were used. It's impossible to tell because nobody wrote anything down in the Bronze Age.

Look!

The giant stones of the Stonehenge stone circle are positioned so that on the longest day and the shortest day of the year (called the solstices) the sun rises exactly between two of the stones.

Stone circles

Towards the end of the Stone Age stone circles were put up around Britain. These were used in the early Bronze Age as well. The circles were aligned (lined up) with the position of the sun in the sky at different times, so perhaps the builders thought the Earth and the sun were connected in a religious way.

The most famous stone circle is at Stonehenge in Wiltshire, which was begun in the Stone Age but was an important sacred site (religious place) during the early Bronze Age.

6

▲ Man-made Silbury Hill.

A mystery mound

Not far from Stonehenge there is a mysterious hill called Silbury Hill. It is the biggest man-made mound in Europe, and it is nearly 40m high. It seems to have been built up gradually, layer by layer, over a long period of time in the early Bronze Age. Tunnels dug into the hill have revealed that nobody was buried inside so what could the hill have been for? Nobody knows!

Code in stone

Cup and ring rock carvings, some from the early Bronze Age, are found scattered around northern England and Scotland. A cup and ring carving is a small cup shape surrounded by circles, carved onto a slab of rock. We have no idea what the shapes symbolise. Perhaps they mark land ownership or sacred places. They are a mystery code we may never crack!

▼ Cup and ring carvings on a rock.

If you lived in the Bronze Age...

In early Bronze Age times you might have made a journey to a sacred stone circle to take part in a ceremony. Perhaps people thought that stone circle ceremonies could influence the sun and help bring good weather for crops to grow.

Find a mine

When metalworking arrived in Britain, people began to make bronze for axes, swords, shields and jewellery. Bronze is an alloy, which means it is a mixture of metals. It is made by heating tin and copper together.

Deep dark work

During the Bronze Age, tin came from Cornwall in the south-west of England, and we now know that much of the copper came from Great Orme, near Llandudno in Wales.

At Great Orme there is a network of hand-dug tunnels for mining copper. ▼

If you lived in the Bronze Age...

If you had worked down the Great Orme mine, life would have been tough and probably short. It was hard to breathe underground and it was freezing cold.

The astonishing Great Orme mine was discovered there in 1987 – nearly 9km of tunnels carved out between 4000 BCE and 1000 BCE by miners toiling in terrible conditions. The narrow tunnels snaked this way and that, following seams of copper ore (layers of rock containing copper) hidden 18m below ground in limestone rock.

Chip, chip, chip

All the copper ore had to be painstakingly dug from the surrounding rocks, using large stones as hammers and cattle bones as picks. The tunnels are so narrow that workers must have been on their hands and knees. They had to kick the copper ore and the waste limestone behind them as they went. Some of the tunnels are so narrow it's likely only children could have worked in them.

Hole at the heart

At the heart of the mine there is an enormous man-made chamber (a giant space). It is the largest hand-made chamber

Look!

Stone hammers and bone picks have been found down the Great Orme mine, dropped there by the Bronze Age miners thousands of years ago.

▲ Stones used to hammer out the tunnels at Great Orme.

in the world, yet it was all hollowed out by people tapping with stones and bones! It's thought the miners gathered around 1,800 tonnes of copper ore from the mine altogether.

Make some bronze

Bronze Age metalworkers were incredibly skilled. Modern craftspeople have tried using ancient techniques and have discovered just how hard it was to make a Bronze Age axehead or sword of just the right weight and shape.

Bronze Age bars

Bronze is usually around 90 per cent copper and 10 per cent tin. To extract the copper and tin from ore (rock), the ore had to be broken into small pieces and then heated over a charcoal fire. The metal became liquid, ran out of the ore, and could then be made into bars called ingots. Copper and tin ingots have been found on a Bronze Age shipwreck off the coast of Salcombe in Devon. It was transporting them around 3,000 years ago when it sank.

Hot stuff

To make an object such as an axehead or a sword a metalworker first had to heat copper and tin together over a

If you lived in the Bronze Age...

A metalworker must have seemed like a magician, pouring glowing hot liquid metal and transforming it into objects. No wonder these objects were used in religious ceremonies (see p26).

Reproductions of Bronze Age axeheads. They would have had wooden handles. ▶

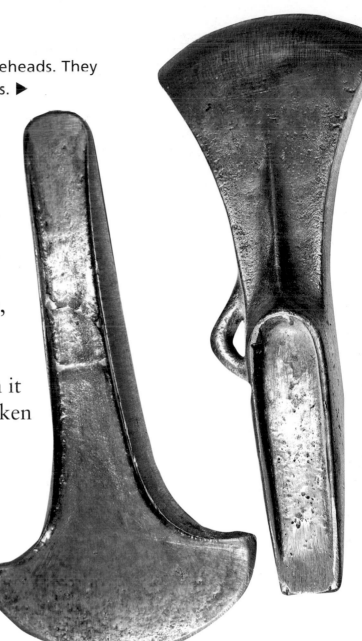

super-hot fire. It would have taken several hours to get the fire hot enough, blowing air on it with bellows made from animal skin. Once the metal had melted and mixed together, it was poured like glowing golden lava into a heated mould made of clay. When it cooled, the mould was broken open to reveal the casting (shape) inside.

Super swords

Bronze Age swords were very light and much smaller than swords made in later times. They were kept beautifully sharp, and experts still haven't worked out just how the ancient craftspeople were able to make such fine blade edges. Swords were probably precious objects owned by only the wealthy important people.

Look!

You can see modern metalsmiths using Bronze Age techniques to make swords and axeheads on *YouTube*.

Meet some leaders

At this time in Britain people lived in groups called tribes. Tribal leaders had the most wealth and were buried in specially built tombs with luxury belongings. Tribes probably owned territory – land they controlled.

Top tombs

At Kilmartin in Scotland there are five surviving early Bronze Age tombs, probably for important people. Each tomb was a box shape lined with big stone slabs, a style of grave called a cist. The cist was hidden under a pile of boulders. Inside the tomb, people were buried with possessions. Perhaps they believed they might need them in an afterlife.

A box-shaped cist tomb at Kilmartin, Scotland. ▼

If you lived in the Bronze Age...

In early to mid Bronze Age times you would have lived alongside the people in your tribe and rarely seen anyone else. There may only have been between 20,000 and 80,000 people in the whole of Britain. Now there are more than 60 million of us!

Count my axes

One of the heavy stone grave-covering slabs at Kilmartin is carved on the underside with pictures of axeheads. These would have faced down on the grave, so it seems they were for the dead person to see. The tribal leaders of Kilmartin were probably rich and powerful because they controlled the main trade routes into Scotland.

Dressed to impress

A Bronze Age burial on the Isle of Bute in Scotland contained over 100 shiny black jet beads that made up a fabulous necklace. Around 4,000 years ago, when it was put into the grave, it would have been a great treasure probably worn by a female tribal leader. She would have impressed everyone who saw her wearing it!

This Bronze Age black jet necklace was worn by an important woman in Scotland. ▼

Look!

Unusually for stone, jet becomes static and attracts dust if it is rubbed (rub an inflated balloon to see the same effect). It's possible that Bronze Age people might have thought it was magical.

Explore a mound

Very little remains of Bronze Age life, which makes graves very important to archaeologists. The things found inside graves provide clues about how people lived.

Moundland

Around 3,500–4,000 years ago many important people were buried in round-shaped mounds. The mounds were often carefully positioned so that they could be seen from a distance. Dorset in south-west England

▲ Winterbourne Poor Lot is full of burial mounds for Bronze Age people.

has the most Bronze Age burial mounds in the whole world, including 44 mounds in one place, called the Winterbourne Poor Lot Barrows.

Sacred spots

Many of the mounds at Poor Lot haven't been excavated, but those that have show that bodies were often cremated (burnt) and the remains were put into clay pots. Food bowls, weapons and tools were put in the mounds too. The richer the person, the finer the objects.

If you lived in the Bronze Age...

You would not have used money in the Bronze Age. Instead you would have given people objects in return for something you wanted – whether that was a promise of help in the future, a crafted object such as jewellery, a share of the harvest or a marriage proposal.

Look!

You may be able to visit Bronze Age burial mounds near where you live. They are dotted around Britain, and finds from them may be in your local museum.

Mold gold

One of the most stunning finds from the whole of the Bronze Age comes from a burial mound in Mold, North Wales. It is a beautiful gold cape, found on the remains of a skeleton. It was finely made and decorated but whoever wore it could not have moved their arms very well, so it was probably only for special ceremonies.

▼ The golden Mold cape.

Paddle a boat

In 1992 an amazing discovery was made in Dover, Kent, when workmen were digging an underpass. A Bronze Age boat came to light for the first time in 3,550 years. It is the oldest sea-going boat in the world.

Freeze-dried find

The Dover Boat had been buried in mud and clay, which had stopped it rotting. But once the boat's timbers were in the open air it was in danger of drying out. Archaeologists had to quickly soak the timbers in liquid wax to preserve them, and then freeze-dry the pieces. Now the boat is on display at the Dover Museum in a special temperature-controlled case.

The oldest sea-going boat in the world, found buried in mud. ▼

If you lived in the Bronze Age...

If you were a powerful Bronze Age person, you probably would have shown off possessions that came from far away as a sign of your importance. Objects brought by boat were quite rare and valuable.

◄ Bronze Age jewellery under the water in a Dorset shipwreck.

Keep bailing!

The boat was made from oak planks sewn together with bendy yew tree shoots called withies. It was around 18m long and big enough to carry cargo. Men used oars to power it along on journeys which were quite dangerous because the boat wasn't watertight!

Broken boat

Archaeologists discovered that the boat had been scuttled (made unusable) around 1150 BCE (just over 3,000 years ago). Some of the withies had been deliberately cut and the front of the boat had been removed. We don't know why, but it's possible it might have been put into a stream as some kind of religious offering. Bronze Age people sometimes put valuable possessions into rivers and lakes (see p26).

Look!

We know that Bronze Age swords, axes and metal ingots were swapped with people abroad, so perhaps the Dover Boat took cargo to and fro across the English Channel. Dover is still a major port for cross-Channel traffic.

Visit a village

During the mid-Bronze Age (around 1500–1000 BCE) people lived in villages for the first time. They built permanent homes alongside their neighbours and survived by farming the land. Remains of fields and homes can still be seen on Dartmoor in Devon.

Farm fields

From the air it is possible to see thousands of straight lines criss-crossing the moor. The lines are called reaves. These were walls made from earth and rubble, marking the boundaries of Bronze Age fields where people once grazed animals and grew crops such as wheat. There are thousands of acres of reaves, so Dartmoor must once have been a very busy Bronze Age community.

Reaves criss-crossing Dartmoor. ▼

Look!

Nobody realised how many reaves there were until aeroplanes began to fly over Dartmoor taking colour photos in the 1970s. Incredible Bronze Age sites such as this are being discovered more and more, thanks to modern technology.

If you lived in the Bronze Age...

By the mid-Bronze Age it would be normal to grow up in the same place as your parents and grandparents and marry your neighbours. Your life would be much more settled than people before you. During the Stone Age people travelled around, following herds of animals to hunt.

▲ The remains of a round Bronze Age home at Grimspound.

Safe for sheep

The houses on Dartmoor were round and built from stone with a turf roof. The remains of 24 homes have been found built together at Grimspound, and we know the people there were farmers because they built stone pens for their animals. All the houses were encircled by a stone wall to keep farm animals in and wild creatures out – bears roamed Dartmoor in the Bronze Age.

Bronze Age days

Ordinary Bronze Age people such as those on Dartmoor were very self-sufficient. They spent their days tending their fields and grinding grain into flour to make a kind of flatbread to eat. They wove their own clothing from wool gathered from their sheep, and made their own tools. They relied on good weather to grow crops. Without it, they risked starvation.

Discover a girl

In 2013 a very rare discovery was made on one of the highest spots on Dartmoor. Hidden under a mound of peat lay a young Bronze Age person with objects that tell us a little about what she wore 3,500 years ago.

Wrapped in fur

It's hard to tell, but the burial was probably a girl aged 15–25. Her body was cremated (burnt) and the burnt bones were wrapped in fur and buried along with a basket containing precious possessions. The fur came from a bear as bears didn't

▲ An archaeologist carefully excavates the Dartmoor burial.

die out in Britain until around 1,000 years ago. We don't know who the girl was or why she had a special burial in such a high-up spot. Perhaps she was from a ruling family.

If you lived in the Bronze Age...

Your clothes were woven from wool or plant fibres. You might have learnt to how to weave cloth and sew your own clothes.

Handmade with care

The girl owned a belt of finely woven fibre made from nettles. Its outer edges were decorated with fringes of tiny leather triangles. She also had a delicate armband made of cow hair plaited with shiny tin beads, rather like a modern beaded friendship bracelet. Her basket was woven with fibres made from lime tree bark, and it looked like the kind of basket you might see today in Africa or India.

Fashionable beads

Beads from a pretty necklace lay scattered in the basket (below). It had clay beads, shale (stone) beads and orange amber beads that came from eastern Europe.

Go inside a home

By around 3,500 years ago things had changed greatly from the time that the Amesbury Archer arrived in Britain. Houses from this period in the Bronze Age have been rebuilt at Flag Fen in Cambridgeshire.

Cosy but dark

We know that there were villages of round-shaped houses at Flag Fen because archaeologists have found post holes – holes in the ground made by the wooden posts used to build the house walls.

Modern copies of Bronze Age houses have been built at Flag Fen. ▼

also found the remains of the first-ever wheel found in Britain. It was made of wood and might have been used on some kind of wooden cart.

This Bronze Age woollen 'beanie' hat was found in Denmark. ▼

In together

Instead of separate rooms, like modern homes, there was just one big room where everybody lived together. Areas of the room were probably set aside for different jobs, such as cooking or weaving. Smoke drifted up through the roof from a fire in the middle of the room. People probably slept on mattress bags stuffed with straw and perhaps used animal skins to keep themselves warm.

The first horses and wheels

We know from things found at Flag Fen that people now had horses to help them with their farming work. Archaeologists

Walk a causeway

Around 3,000 years ago the weather in Britain grew much wetter. Farming must have become much harder. The people at low-lying Flag Fen in Cambridgeshire had to contend with flooding, but they built a causeway to cope with the rising waters.

Staking out a walkway

The causeway ran across the watery fenland. It was made by driving more than 60,000 sharpened wooden stakes into the ground in long lines, with planks on top. In the middle there was a wide platform, like a wooden island, above the water.

◀ Today, modern stakes mark the route of the ancient causeway.

Look!

Timbers from the ancient causeway have survived, and they are now preserved at Flag Fen. Visitors can see them along with lots of the objects that were mysteriously thrown into the water.

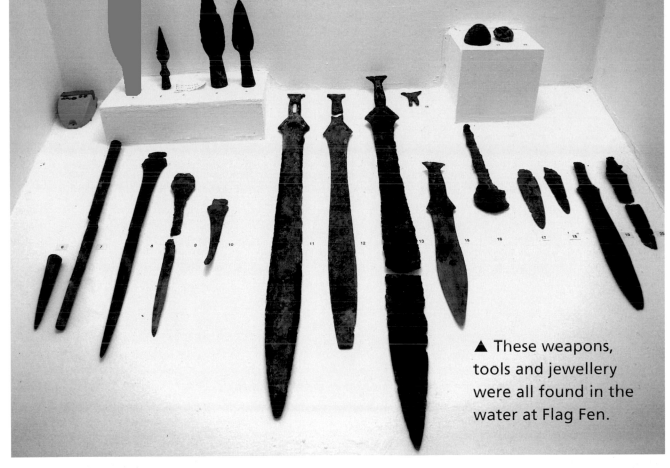

▲ These weapons, tools and jewellery were all found in the water at Flag Fen.

Secrets of the water

People threw all kinds of valuable things into the water from the causeway, including swords, gold jewellery and tools. Some of the offerings had been deliberately broken. People also threw in white beach pebbles, brought from far away. They must have thought these were special, perhaps even magical.

Water power

We can make a guess that the platform in the centre of the causeway was built for ceremonies and that the valuable items were hurled into the water as religious offerings. It's thought that people may have believed that water was a way into an underworld where magical spirits lived.

If you lived in the Bronze Age...

Because everybody grew their own food, bad weather led to shortages and perhaps even famine. Life towards the end of the Bronze Age seemed to be getting tougher!

Hide a hoard

We call the period from 1000 BCE onwards the late Bronze Age in Britain. It's a strange time that leaves us with lots of puzzling questions!

▲ Pieces from a Bronze Age horse harness found at Llyn Fawr.

Buried secrets

All over late Bronze Age Britain people began burying valuable objects or throwing them in water, more often than ever before. We have no idea why. Perhaps there was famine or fighting across the land, and people were either making extra religious offerings or hiding their possessions. Some of the objects were hidden in big collections called hoards.

Water hoard

When workmen were building a reservoir at Llyn Fawr in Wales in 1911–12, they uncovered a hoard of over 60 objects that had been thrown in a

If you lived in the Bronze Age...

If you lived in the late Bronze Age, you probably knew a greater number of people than your early Bronze Age ancestors. There were now around 500,000 people living in Britain, and there were lots of villages dotted around the country.

lake around 750–600 BCE. The hoard included lots of tools, a big cauldron and some bronze razors for shaving (it seems Bronze Age men did not like having beards). We don't know who put the hoard in the lake. It might have been a local tribe.

New metal

Two of the objects in the Llyn Fawr hoard are very rare and unusual for the time: a sickle (a farm tool) and a sword made of iron. These are some of the oldest iron objects ever found in Britain. Iron was only just being used and hardly any has been found from before 550 BCE. But iron ore, used to make iron, is cheap and easy to find. It was about to replace bronze as the commonest metal in Britain.

▲ The hoard was found at the bottom of the original smaller lake at Llyn Fawr.

Look!

The Llyn Fawr cauldron would probably have been a treasured object, and may have been used in religious ceremonies. It is so big that you would not have been able to get your arms around it!

Carve a horse

High on a Wiltshire hillside there is a puzzling picture of a giant horse created by our ancestors 3,000 years ago.

Horse of chalk

The white horse at Uffington was made by carving trenches in the hill and filling them with chalk. It is 110m long, and it is near one of Britain's most ancient pathways, the Ridgeway Track, which runs all the way from the west country to the east coast. The horse has been dated to around 1000 BCE, and local people have been looking after it ever since. For 30 centuries they have made sure the grass did not grow over the picture!

The Uffington white horse, carved into the ground on a hillside. ▼

Look!

By now horses had become much more important in Britain, for both working and for riding. Soon they would gallop into battle, pulling Iron Age warriors in war chariots.

Weapons from the Iron Age, the very latest technology 2,800 years ago. ▶

Here comes the Iron Age

Near the horse there is a big hill fort of banks and ditches. It was built in the Iron Age, the period of history that began around 800–700 BCE in Britain. In this new era tribes hid in their hill-top strongholds and fought with each other using iron weapons.

What does it mean?

The horse might have been a tribal badge that showed travellers who owned the land they walked on. Or it might have been a religious symbol. We know that a horse goddess was worshipped in the Iron Age, so perhaps it represented the new religion of the local people.

If you lived in the Bronze Age...

In this ancient world you would never have said 'This is the Bronze Age' or 'Now this is the Iron Age'. The names have been created by modern historians. Our ancestors would have had no idea what they meant!

Glossary

Alloy A mixture of metals.

Archaeologist Someone who studies history by studying remains left behind.

Bartering A system of swapping goods or services without using money.

Bellows A set of bags that fan the flames of a fire.

Bronze Age Around 2500 BCE to 700 BCE, when people had bronze tools, weapons and jewellery.

Causeway A pathway built above water.

Copper A soft metal extracted from copper ore (rocks containing copper).

Cremation The ceremonial burning of a dead body.

Extract To take something out of something else. Metal is extracted from rocks.

Hoard A collection of objects that has been hidden away.

Ingot A bar of metal.

Ore Rock from which metal is extracted.

Pick A tool used for hitting rock.

Reaves Bronze Age field walls made from soil and rubble.

Ridgeway An ancient trackway that linked western England to eastern England.

Solstice The shortest or longest day of the year.

Stone circle A ring of standing stones where Stone Age and early Bronze Age people may have held religious ceremonies.

Tin A soft metal that comes from tin-carrying rocks.

Trade Buying and selling.

Tunic A simple top, which usually reached from the shoulders to a length somewhere between the hips and the ankles.

Wattles Branches woven together to make a fence or the wall of a house.

Wood turning Shaping wood using a tool called a lathe.